Table o

ISBN 9798884221604

Notice to Readers:

Welcome to the world of humor and satire presented in this book. Before you embark on this journey of laughter and merriment, please take a moment to understand the nature of this content: *Satirical Content*: This book is a work of satire, intended solely for entertainment purposes. It's akin to a literary whoopee cushion, designed to induce laughter and amusement. *Not Professional Advice*: The content herein does not constitute professional advice of any kind, be it medical, therapeutic, or life coaching. It is purely for fun and should not be taken seriously. *Discretion Advised*: If you find the humor or content inappropriate or not to your taste, please exercise your discretion. This book might not be suitable for all audiences. *No Practical Implementation*: The ideas, jokes, and content in this book are not meant to be implemented or acted upon. They are for reading enjoyment only. It's a source of laughter, not a guide for action. *Financial Limitation of Liability*: We, the author(s) and publisher(s) of this book, hold zero financial responsibility for any outcomes, direct or indirect, resulting from the interpretation or use of the contents of this book. This includes any form of financial compensation or reimbursement. *Use at Your Own Risk*: Any attempt to apply or enact scenarios or suggestions from this book is entirely at the reader's risk. The author(s) and publisher(s) assume no responsibility for any consequences that may arise from such actions.

By continuing to read and enjoy this book, you, as the reader, acknowledge and accept this disclaimer, recognizing the book's purpose as a source of humor and acknowledging the financial limitation of liability.

Enjoy the read, but remember – it's meant to tickle your funny bone, not to guide your life decisions.

on Amazon Music, Spotify, Apple Podcasts, and more

the art of

UNDER ACHIEVE MENT

podcast

Let's meet amongst the comfortable cushions and soft sofas of not-so-mediocre **podcast platforms**.

Search for _The Art of Underachievement by Maxwell Easeley_

on Amazon Music, Spotify, Apple Podcasts, and more

the art of

UNDER
ACHIEVE
MENT ☺

podcast

01
Intro

In a world that relentlessly pursues excellence, where success is the yardstick by which we measure our worth, there emerges a need for a different narrative—a narrative that celebrates the overlooked beauty of mediocrity, the unsung melody of underachievement. "The Art of Underachievement – Embracing Mediocrity in a World Obsessed with Success" is a manifesto for the average, a tome that revels in the joy of the unremarkable, offering a counterpoint to the chorus of self-improvement that dominates our cultural landscape.

This book is an invitation to wander through the garden of existence with lighter steps, to lower the bar and find peace beneath it. It champions the art of starting projects without the burden of finishing them, of setting goals with the gentle flexibility of not pursuing them, and of finding contentment in the comfort zone without the constant push to escape it. Through a series of demotivational affirmations and disappointing wisdom, it crafts a space where underachievement is not a failure but a choice, a realm where the pressure of productivity yields to the tranquil embrace of procrastination and the sweet liberation of lowered expectations. Each chapter, each affirmation, serves as a reminder that in the pursuit of average, there lies a profound freedom—a freedom from the tyranny of ambition, a liberation from the relentless pursuit of more. It's a guide to finding joy in the ordinary, to celebrating the stillness of stagnation, and to savoring the simple act of being rather than the complex art of becoming.

So, as you turn these pages, allow yourself to be enveloped in the comforting blanket of mediocrity, to bask in the glow of unfulfilled potential, and to find solace in the fact that in the grand tapestry of life, being just OK is not just OK—it's enough.

02

The fine art of never finishing anything – a guide to starting projects you'll never complete.

Embarking on a new project is like standing on the precipice of possibility, the horizon brimming with the promise of what could be. Yet, there exists a sublime artistry in the act of beginning without the intention, or perhaps the burden, of completion. This chapter celebrates the fine art of never finishing anything, a guide to those first exhilarating steps into new endeavors that are destined to remain forever unfinished. It's a toast to the potential, to the beauty of beginnings, and the freedom found in leaving things incomplete.

To start is to dream, to embark on a journey without the constraints of a destination. Each new project is a canvas upon which we paint our initial strokes of enthusiasm and creativity, where the thrill of the new is unmarred by the weight of completion. In this space, the pressure to perfect is absent, and the joy of creation is untainted by the eventual judgement of the final product. Here, we find liberation in the perpetual state of in-progress, a testament to our ever-evolving nature and the fluidity of our aspirations. This is not about the failure to finish but the courage to begin, again and again, embracing each start as an end in itself. The unfinished projects we accumulate are not markers of defeat but badges of honor, celebrating our willingness to explore, to experiment, and to engage with the process without being shackled by the outcome. They are reminders that in the art of living, it is the journey that matters, the series of beginnings that weave the tapestry of our lives, rich with the threads of attempted ventures and the colors of unrealized dreams.

Why finish what you start when you can savor the mystery of what could have been?

Why indeed rush to the finish line when the race itself is dotted with so many delightful distractions? After all, the journey is where the magic happens, or so they say when they're too tired to reach the end.

Imagine for a moment the projects you've started with the fire of a thousand suns, only to leave them simmering on the back burner of your ambition. Each unfinished task is not a sign of failure, but a testament to your limitless potential and, let's be honest, your equally limitless ability to be distracted by literally anything else. There's a certain charm in wondering what could have been, a sort of Schrödinger's project where, as long as you don't finish it, it could theoretically have been a masterpiece. Besides, in the museum of your mind, these unfinished masterpieces are forever preserved in their most pristine state: perfect in potential, untainted by the cruel brush of reality. Let's not forget, every time you don't finish something, you're also not failing at it – and in today's competitive world, that's practically a win. So, as you gaze upon your kingdom of half-done wonders, remember that in the grand tapestry of life, these are the threads that sparkle with the most intriguing possibilities.

Because, at the end of the day, it's not about the projects we complete, but about the stories we tell around the ones we didn't. And isn't that mystery just a little bit more interesting?

Starting projects is a form of art; completing them is just overrated.

In the grand gallery of life, starting projects is like sketching with bold, daring strokes on a canvas, each line brimming with potential and promise. Completing them, though? That's where the art critics step in, and who needs that kind of scrutiny?

Every new beginning is a masterpiece waiting to happen, a fresh page in the novel of your potential greatness. It's the rush of excitement, the thrill of creation, that intoxicates you, not the mundane satisfaction of tying up loose ends. As you leap from project to project, you're not being fickle or unfocused; you're curating an eclectic exhibition of what-ifs and might-have-beens. Each abandoned endeavor is a testament to your adventurous spirit, a sign that you're too creative, too dynamic to be bogged down by something as pedestrian as completion. After all, the world is full of finishers, but it's the starters who bring the spark, the ones who ignite the flames of inspiration and then, wisely, let others handle the burnout. Why chain yourself to the tyranny of the endgame when you can be free to chase the next big thing, the next exhilarating start?

So let's not belittle the unfinished; let's celebrate it as the highest form of artistic expression. After all, isn't life too short to spend it crossing T's and dotting I's?

Embrace the chaos of unfinished tasks – they're the true monuments to your potential.

In a world obsessed with the destination, there's something rebelliously beautiful about cherishing the journey, especially when it's scattered with the ruins of what could have been. Unfinished tasks? No, they're not mere reminders of procrastination; they're grand monuments to your boundless potential.

Each unfinished task is like an open-ended story, a novel without a final chapter that leaves its ending to the imagination of its beholder. These monuments stand tall, not as symbols of failure, but as beacons of possibility, each one a testament to the myriad paths your creativity can take. They are the tangible proof that your ambition knows no bounds, that your drive to start anew is a force of nature unto itself. In the chaos of these unfinished symphonies lies a harmony of sorts, a melody that sings of the courage to explore, to begin, and to dream without the chains of conclusion. This collection of half-built castles and uncompleted bridges maps out the landscape of your mind, where every incomplete task holds a story, a lesson, or a dream momentarily paused but never truly abandoned. They remind us that in the pursuit of greatness, the act of creation itself is an achievement, a sign that we dared to dream, to do, to be.

So, embrace the clutter of your ambitions as the truest representation of your potential. After all, it's the unfinished symphonies that often have the most beautiful melodies.

. . .

As we close the cover on this chapter of perpetual beginnings, let's carry forward the understanding that the fine art of never finishing anything is, in its essence, a celebration of life's infinite possibilities. It's an acknowledgment that not all paths need to be followed to their end, that there's beauty and value in the act of starting, even without the closure of completion. So, here's to the starters, the dreamers, the eternal initiators—may your projects be as boundless as your imagination, and may you find joy in the art of beginning, for it is in the act of starting that we are most alive. After all, the world is full of finishers, but it's the ones who keep starting who truly paint the broad strokes of innovation and change.

03

Celebrating the comfort zone – why stretch when you can rest?

In a world that constantly champions the mantra of "push your limits," there exists a counter-narrative, a serene call to arms (or perhaps, a call to relax those arms) that celebrates the sanctity of the comfort zone. This chapter is not an ode to stagnation but a tribute to the beauty of finding and appreciating one's own space of optimal existence—where the heart beats in rhythm with contentment, and the mind is at peace with the familiar. Why stretch into the uncomfortable when you can rest in the bliss of your personal sanctuary?

The comfort zone, often maligned as the graveyard of ambition, is, in truth, a garden of self-awareness and self-acceptance. It's where we know the contours of our abilities and the limits of our desires. Here, in this familiar landscape, there's no need for the constant strain of becoming, for the relentless pursuit of more. Instead, there's an appreciation for what is, for the moments of simple joys and the ease of well-worn routines. This isn't about refusing growth but about recognizing that not all growth requires discomfort or a leap into the unknown. Sometimes, the most profound expansions happen quietly, gently, within the bounds of our comfort zones, where we're free to explore, experiment, and express ourselves without the fear of failure or the pressure of expectations. It's in this space that creativity can bloom from a place of security, and happiness can flourish in the soil of familiarity. The comfort zone is not a trap but a basecamp, a foundation from which we can venture out when we choose and to which we can always return.

Why step out of your comfort zone when you can decorate it with mediocrity?

Why indeed venture into the unpredictable wilds beyond your comfort zone when the cozy confines of your familiar space await, ripe for adornment with the fine tapestries of mediocrity? Stepping out might offer growth, but staying in promises the warm embrace of the known, no surprises, just the comforting hum of the status quo.

In the grand scheme of life, venturing beyond the comfort zone is touted as the path to greatness, a necessary leap towards self-improvement. Yet, there's an unspoken charm in the embrace of mediocrity, a serene acceptance of one's place in the grand mosaic of existence without the relentless pursuit of more. Here, in the comfort zone, every corner is a testament to the things that are "good enough," where ambitions are not doused but softly lulled into a gentle, undisturbed slumber. This is where the pressure to excel dissipates into the ether, replaced by the soft, reassuring whisper of contentment. Decorating this space with mediocrity doesn't mean giving up; it's an art form—a celebration of life's simpler achievements. After all, in the relentless pursuit of excellence, one risks missing out on the small, perfect moments of joy found in the average, the mundane, the utterly mediocre.

So, let's raise a glass to the splendidly average, to the art of adorning our comfort zones with the plush, velvety layers of just-enough. Because why strive for the stars when the soft glow of the nightlight is enough to illuminate our world?

Stretching your limits is a risk. Embrace the safety of the familiar pillow fort.

In an age where the mantra of pushing boundaries is echoed from every mountaintop and motivational poster, there's a whispered wisdom in the embrace of the familiar, the safety of our personal pillow forts. Why risk the unknown when the known is so wonderfully comforting?

Venturing beyond one's comfort zone is often painted as the ultimate act of courage, a testament to one's adventurous spirit. Yet, there's an underrated valor in recognizing the beauty of where you are, in the warmth of the well-trodden path, the softness of the familiar. The pillow fort, a bastion of security crafted from the cushions of routine and the blankets of predictability, stands as a monument to the peace found in the unchallenged, the unchanged. Here, in the cocoon of the known, risks are minimized, and the heart beats to the rhythm of contented regularity. The world outside, with its sharp corners and unpredictable storms, offers growth, yes, but at what cost? Inside the pillow fort, every element is curated for comfort, each pillow placed with care to support, not challenge. It's a reminder that sometimes, the greatest adventures are found not in the stretching of limits, but in the deep exploration of the landscapes we already inhabit.

So, let's not hastily abandon the sanctuary of our pillow forts in the pursuit of distant horizons. After all, the greatest risk might just be missing the profound joy hidden in the heart of the familiar.

Your comfort zone: Where dreams gently expire, so you don't have to chase them.

Ah, the comfort zone, that softly padded cell where dreams come to rest, nestled among the cushions of routine and the familiar. It's a place so cozy, so ensconcing, that aspirations merely whisper before tucking themselves in for a long, undisturbed nap.

Within the confines of this sanctuary, dreams are not so much chased as they are courteously escorted to a plush armchair, offered a warm cup of tea, and gently persuaded to stay awhile—forever, if they like. Here, ambition morphs into a quiet contentment, a serene acceptance of what is, rather than an insatiable hunger for what could be. The comfort zone offers a tranquil sea, where the waves of desire softly lap against the shores of satisfaction, never too eager to disturb the peace. It's a realm where the pursuit of greatness takes a backseat to the simple pleasures of being, where the ladder of success is replaced by a cozy hammock, swaying gently in the breeze of complacency. In this haven, the fear of failure is a distant memory, obscured by the fog of comfortable routine. The beauty of the comfort zone lies not in the dreams that die within its walls, but in the peaceful surrender to a life unburdened by the relentless chase.

So, let's celebrate the comfort zone, a place where dreams don't die; they simply retire early, leaving us to enjoy the quiet, unremarkable bliss of the here and now. After all, in the race of life, sometimes the best move is to quietly bow out and let the dreams sleep in.

• • •

As we wrap up this celebration of the comfort zone, let's dispel the myth that staying within it is a sign of weakness or a lack of ambition. On the contrary, it's a testament to knowing oneself, to understanding one's own needs and limits. It's about finding balance in a world that often feels off-kilter with its demands and expectations. So, cherish your comfort zone, nurture it, and know that in the grand adventure of life, it's not just about the distance traveled but the quality of the journey. Why stretch when you can rest? Because sometimes, the greatest adventures are found not in the places we go, but in the depths of our own inner landscapes, comfortably explored from our favorite spot in the world.

04

Aim for the stars, land on the couch – the gravitational pull of low expectations.

I n the vast universe of ambition, where "aim for the stars" is the rallying cry of the motivated, there exists a cozy, uncharted space where expectations gently settle like dust on an old bookshelf: the couch. This chapter isn't about failing to reach the stars due to lack of trying but rather about the blissful surrender to the gravitational pull of low expectations. It's a journey from the dizzying heights of potential to the comforting embrace of the living room couch, where dreams adjust to the cozy contours of reality.

The voyage from the stars to the couch is not one of defeat; it's a celestial recalibration, where the pressures of cosmic ambition give way to the serene acceptance of earthly pleasures. Here, in the soft glow of the television screen or the immersive depth of a good book, ambitions aren't lost; they're merely transformed into something more manageable, more immediate, and infinitely more comfortable. This gravitational pull towards lower expectations isn't a failure of will but a conscious choice to find joy in the simpler, quieter aspects of life. It's an acknowledgment that while the stars may offer a glittering tapestry of possibilities, the couch offers a familiar, nurturing space where we can recharge, reflect, and perhaps dream anew, albeit on a less grandiose scale. In this transition, we learn the art of adjusting our sails, not to catch the winds of fortune but to drift along the currents of contentment. The couch becomes not just a piece of furniture but a vessel, carrying us through the tranquil seas of self-acceptance, where the only expectation is to be at peace with oneself and one's place in the universe.

Aim for the stars, but remember, couches don't have gravity.

Aiming for the stars, they say, is the epitome of ambition, a testament to the human spirit's boundless capacity to dream. But amidst this celestial striving, let's not forget a fundamental truth: couches, those trusty bastions of comfort, remain blissfully unaffected by gravity's demanding grip.

In the cosmic ballet of aspiration and reality, there's a quaint charm in acknowledging the gravitational pull of the couch. It's more than a piece of furniture; it's a sanctuary, a ground control of sorts for our star-bound ambitions. Here, in the soft embrace of its cushions, dreams of interstellar achievements gently collide with the comforting inertia of rest. This isn't to say that the stars are beyond our reach; rather, it's an invitation to appreciate the joy in the journey, the moments of pause, the zero-gravity experience of doing absolutely nothing. The couch offers a unique perspective on ambition, one where looking up at the stars doesn't necessitate leaving the comfort of our earthly confines. It's a reminder that sometimes, the most profound discoveries are made not in the vacuum of space, but in the warm, quiet moments of reflection that only a couch can provide. In this gentle orbit around our living rooms, we find that our most cherished dreams and ambitions can coexist with a peaceful, grounded contentment.

So, by all means, aim for the stars—but don't underestimate the cosmic allure of the couch, where dreams float freely, unencumbered by the harsh realities of gravity. After all, in the vast expanse of the universe, what's more human than finding our own little corner of gravity-free bliss?

Shooting for the moon is hard; landing back on your sofa is guaranteed.

Shooting for the moon, that age-old metaphor for reaching beyond our grasp, embodies the pinnacle of human aspiration. Yet, in the shadow of such lofty endeavors lies a comforting, undeniable truth: the return journey to your sofa is a foregone conclusion, a sweet, gravitational pull back to the familiar and the easy.

The moon represents the ultimate in achievement, a celestial target that dares us to defy our limitations and venture into the unknown. However, this cosmic quest, while noble, overlooks the simple pleasures waiting at the mission's end. As we don our metaphorical spacesuits, plotting trajectories that stretch our capabilities to their limits, the sofa waits patiently, offering a soft landing pad for when the fuel of ambition runs low. There's a profound beauty in this cycle of aspiration and return, a reminder that every grand adventure is bookended by moments of rest and reflection. The sofa, in its unassuming way, serves as a grounding force, a reminder that no matter how far we reach, the comforts of home provide a sanctuary for recovery and contemplation. It's here, in the familiar embrace of our living rooms, that we're free to dream anew, cushioned against the hard landings of reality. This isn't to suggest that aiming for the moon isn't a worthy endeavor, but rather to celebrate the journey's end as much as its beginning. After all, the greatest explorations are those that bring us back to ourselves, to our own cozy corner of the universe.

So, while the moon might offer the allure of the unknown, never underestimate the gravitational comfort of your sofa, where every return is a gentle reminder that the most important landings are the ones that bring us home.

Why reach for the stars when the remote control is much closer?

In the grand tapestry of human ambition, the stars have always represented the ultimate frontier, a celestial challenge to our innate desire to explore and conquer. Yet, in the comfort of our own living rooms, a profound question emerges from the depths of the couch: why reach for the stars when the remote control is so tantalizingly close?

This isn't just a question of physical proximity; it's a philosophical inquiry into the nature of our aspirations. The remote control, within arm's reach, embodies the immediate gratification of our modern existence, offering a universe of entertainment with the mere press of a button. Why embark on the arduous journey towards distant dreams when a world of escapism lies nestled in the palm of your hand? This juxtaposition between celestial ambition and terrestrial comfort invites us to reconsider our priorities, to find a balance between the pursuit of the extraordinary and the appreciation of the mundane. The remote control, in its humble simplicity, challenges the notion that fulfillment must always lie beyond the next horizon, suggesting instead that contentment might be found in the here and now. It's a reminder that while the stars may inspire us with their distant glow, there's also beauty to be found in the small, everyday moments that make up our lives. In this light, the act of reaching for the remote becomes not a symbol of surrender, but a choice to embrace the immediate, to celebrate the accessible, and to find joy in the effortless.

So, the next time you find yourself gazing upward, dreaming of the stars, remember that sometimes the most satisfying journeys are those we can embark upon without ever leaving the couch. After all, why stretch for the stars when the remote control offers a universe of possibilities at your fingertips?

. . .

As we conclude this chapter on the gravitational pull of low expectations, let us embrace the couch not as a symbol of unfulfilled potential but as a sanctuary of self-compassion and realism. In the cosmic ballet of ambition and satisfaction, there's grace in allowing oneself to land softly, cushioned by the understanding that not all journeys need to be epic to be meaningful. So, aim for the stars, by all means, but remember, landing on the couch doesn't mean you've given up on the cosmos; it simply means you've found a comfortable spot from which to admire them. After all, in the grand scheme of things, a contented soul on the couch is worth more than all the stars in the sky.

05

Mastering the art of minimal effort – doing just enough to not get fired.

In the high-octane world of career advancement and professional growth, there exists a lesser-known, quietly celebrated craft: mastering the art of minimal effort. This is not the tale of laziness nor of mediocrity, but rather a strategic guide to navigating the choppy waters of employment with the grace of a swan—serene on the surface but paddling just enough underneath to keep moving. As we explore this chapter, we'll delve into the nuanced art of doing just enough to not get fired, a balancing act between efficiency and effortlessness that champions the beauty of "just right."

The adept practitioner of minimal effort understands that this art is grounded in the keen perception of value—distinguishing between what must be done excellently and what simply needs to be done. It's a dance of prioritization, where energy is allocated not by the demands of the task but by the task's visibility and impact. This sage warrior wields the weapon of selective excellence, choosing battles with the precision of a chess grandmaster, ensuring that when it counts, they shine, and when it doesn't, they blend into the background with practiced nonchalance. This philosophy extends beyond mere survival; it's a form of professional judo, using the momentum of workplace dynamics to maintain position with minimal exertion. By mastering the art of minimal effort, one not only conserves energy but also cultivates an aura of calm efficiency, a mirage that often deflects scrutiny and demands. The key lies in the subtle art of delegation, automation, and the strategic embrace of "good enough," allowing one to navigate the tightrope of expectations with the grace of a tightrope walker—always balanced, never overreaching.

Putting in maximum effort means more things can go wrong. Aim for 'just enough'.

In a world that champions the maxim, "Go big or go home," there's a subtle art to aiming for 'just enough', a strategic finesse in navigating the tightrope of effort where the safety net is woven from threads of pragmatism and peace of mind. After all, when you commit to giving it your all, you're not just investing effort; you're also multiplying the chances for things to spectacularly derail.

The beauty of 'just enough' lies in its understated elegance, the perfect balance between doing and overdoing. It's a philosophy that appreciates the merit in moderation, understanding that sometimes, the best outcome is one that requires the least repair. This isn't about shirking responsibility or advocating for mediocrity; rather, it's recognizing that in the vast landscape of potential pitfalls, there's wisdom in navigating a path that minimizes risk while still reaching the destination. By aiming for 'just enough', you're not tempering ambition; you're refining it, choosing to invest your energies where they yield the highest return with the lowest chance of complication. It's a strategy that champions efficiency over extravagance, that finds virtue in the measured over the maximal. In doing so, you safeguard not just your project's success, but your mental well-being, preserving the bandwidth to appreciate the fruits of your labor without the shadow of what-could-have-beens looming large.

So, let's toast to the brilliance of 'just enough', a guiding principle for those who navigate the world with a keen eye for the optimal, the sustainable, and the gracefully sufficient. After all, why risk a spectacular mess when the beauty of balance offers a smoother ride?

Why be a workhorse when you can be a barely functional decorative pony?

In the grand pageant of life's endless race, where the air is thick with the dust of relentless ambition, there emerges a whisper, a question that floats gently above the fray: Why be a workhorse, tirelessly toiling, when the role of a barely functional decorative pony offers a far more enticing script?

This isn't a call to laziness, nor an ode to underachievement, but rather an invitation to reassess our roles in the spectacle of productivity. The workhorse is admired, yes, for its steadfast resolve, its unwavering dedication to the task at hand. Yet, in the shadow of such Herculean effort, the decorative pony prances—a beacon of light-heartedness amidst the grind. This pony, while perhaps not the engine driving progress forward, serves as a reminder of the joy in simply being. It's in the ornamental, the seemingly superfluous, where we find the spaces to breathe, to laugh, to dance. Here, in the guise of the decorative pony, is the subtle rebellion against the cult of overwork, a declaration that not all value is measured in output, that sometimes the greatest contribution we can make is to adorn the day with a touch of whimsy, a spark of delight. This role, understated yet profound, champions the art of the unnecessary, the beauty of the extraneous, reminding us that in the tapestry of existence, it's the splashes of color, the flourishes of creativity, that truly captivate.

So, the next time the race feels relentless, remember: the world needs its decorative ponies just as much as its workhorses. Why strain under the yoke of perpetual productivity when you can trot into the hearts of others as a reminder that there's more to life than just running the race? After all, isn't life a little brighter with a bit of decorative flair?

Excellence is a lot of pressure. Mediocrity gives you room to breathe... and nap.

In the relentless pursuit of excellence, where every moment is a battle in the war against the ordinary, there lies a suffocating pressure, a weight that demands constant vigilance and effort. Yet, in the gentle embrace of mediocrity, there's a liberating expanse, a verdant field where the air is lighter, the sky a bit bluer, and the promise of a nap tantalizingly within reach.

Excellence, with its glittering allure, is a demanding mistress, always asking for more, pushing you to the brink of your capabilities. It's a realm where the applause is loud but the nights are long, where the pedestal is high but the fall is terrifying. In contrast, mediocrity is like a comfortable, well-worn sofa—it might not impress many, but it offers a cozy nook for your soul to curl up and rest. Here, in this unassuming space, the race against oneself slows to a gentle stroll, where the views can be enjoyed, and the pressures of perfection fade into the background. This isn't about celebrating laziness or lack of ambition, but rather about finding a balance, a humane pace of life where breathing is easy and sleep is sweet. Mediocrity, much maligned by societies obsessed with the best, offers a sanctuary for the majority, a place where you can be good enough and that's perfectly okay. It's a reminder that in the grand scheme of things, being average means you're on par with the vast expanse of humanity, and there's comfort in that shared experience.

So, let's not shy away from mediocrity, from the beautiful, restful plateau where excellence is a view, not a burden. After all, in the endless quest for greatness, sometimes the bravest thing you can do is take a breath... and maybe a nap.

• • •

As we close this chapter on the art of minimal effort, let it be known that this path is not for the faint of heart. It requires a sharp mind, a keen eye for detail, and a profound understanding of the human condition. To walk this line between doing just enough and not getting fired is to embrace a deeper wisdom about work, value, and life itself. So, to the aspiring minimalists in the workforce, may you find your balance, perfect your craft, and discover the peaceful waters that lie beyond the rapids of exertion. After all, in the grand scheme of things, mastering the art of minimal effort is not just about surviving the workplace; it's about thriving within it, one perfectly calculated stroke at a time.

06

The beauty of not trying – letting life happen one binge at a time.

I n a society that often equates success with constant effort and relentless ambition, there exists a serene counterpoint: the beauty of not trying. This philosophy, far from advocating for apathy, invites us to experience life's journey with a sense of ease and acceptance, allowing the moments to unfold naturally, one binge at a time. As we delve into this chapter, we explore the subtle art of letting go, of finding joy and contentment in the simple act of being rather than the relentless pursuit of doing.

There's a certain magic in the act of not trying, a gentle grace in allowing life to flow at its own pace. In this state of effortless being, each experience, from the mundane to the extraordinary, is savored without the burden of expectation. Here, in the realm of unhurried existence, we find freedom in

35

the pauses, the spaces between efforts, where life breathes and blooms in unexpected ways. The beauty of not trying doesn't mean we cease to move forward; rather, it means we move with the current of life, not against it. It's in this dance with the spontaneous that we discover the richness of the present, finding depth and satisfaction in what we might have once overlooked in our haste to achieve. This approach to life, one binge at a time —be it episodes of our favorite show, chapters of a captivating book, or hours spent in leisurely pursuit of happiness—reminds us that there's profound wisdom in simplicity, in the choice to experience rather than to conquer. It teaches us that in the vast tapestry of existence, our most memorable moments often come not from striving, but from simply being.

Embrace the flow of life's stream; let each binge wash over you like a gentle wave.

In the relentless pursuit of purpose and productivity, there's a singular, often overlooked wisdom in letting go, in allowing the gentle currents of life to guide you from one binge to the next. It's a soft surrender to the ebb and flow of existence, where each moment is embraced with the ease of a leaf floating downstream.

This philosophy isn't a call to apathy but an invitation to trust in the journey, to believe that sometimes, the best path forward is the one that unfolds with the least resistance. By letting each binge wash over you, you're not giving up control; you're acknowledging that some of the most beautiful experiences come from simply being present and open to where the stream of life might take you. It's in these moments of surrender that we often find clarity, as the waters of life carry us past the noise and haste, offering perspectives anew. The binges, be they shows, books, or moments of indulgence, become not a means of escape but a way to connect more deeply with ourselves and the world around us. They remind us that life doesn't always have to be about striving and achieving; sometimes, it's about floating and being. In this gentle acceptance of life's flow, we find a peace that comes not from conquering the stream but from becoming one with it.

So, let go and let the stream carry you. Who knows what shores of insight and contentment you might gently wash upon?

In the realm of relaxation, effortlessness is your crown and each binge, your scepter.

In the kingdom of calm and the dominion of downtime, there exists a noble truth: effortlessness is not merely a state of being, but a crown jewel, a regal testament to the art of relaxation. Here, each binge serves not as a sign of idleness but as a scepter, a symbol of sovereignty over one's own time and pleasure.

This regal approach to leisure challenges the conventional valor of exertion, proposing instead that true mastery lies in the ability to revel in the ease of doing nothing with absolute intent. It's a celebration of the choice to indulge, to immerse oneself fully in the pleasures of the present without the shadow of guilt. In this realm, every episode watched, every page turned, and every bite savored is a declaration of dominion over one's own realm of relaxation. This isn't about shunning responsibility but about understanding that in the tapestry of life, threads of rest and enjoyment are essential to the broader picture of well-being. The act of binging, then, becomes a ritual, a ceremonial embrace of joy that recharges the spirit and fortifies the soul. By crowning oneself with effortlessness and wielding each binge as a scepter, one asserts the right to rest, to joy, and to personal peace in a world that often demands the opposite.

So, wear your crown of effortlessness with pride, and let your scepter of bingeing proclaim your right to relaxation and joy. In the end, the realm of relaxation is not for the weary but for the wise.

Let life unfold in episodes; savor the pause between seasons as much as the cliffhangers.

In the grand series of existence, where each day dawns as a new episode filled with plot twists and turns, there's a profound beauty in allowing life to unfold in its episodic nature. It's an invitation to view our journey as a series, complete with season finales and the suspenseful waits in between.

Embracing life in episodes encourages us to appreciate the narrative arcs, the character developments, and the unexpected cliffhangers with a sense of anticipation and acceptance. Each season of our lives brings its own themes, challenges, and triumphs, making the storyline rich and multidimensional. The pause between seasons—those moments of transition and reflection—are just as crucial to our story as the action-packed episodes. They offer a chance to catch our breath, to ponder the lessons learned, and to speculate about the coming adventures. This perspective allows us to approach each new chapter with curiosity rather than anxiety, to savor the unfolding of events with the patience of a seasoned viewer who trusts the storytelling process. These intermissions, these pauses between seasons, are not voids but spaces filled with potential, where the seeds of future episodes germinate in the soil of contemplation and rest. By savoring these pauses as much as the cliffhangers, we cultivate a deeper appreciation for the narrative complexity of our lives, recognizing that every moment, whether dramatic or quiet, contributes to the richness of our personal saga.

So, let's cherish the season finales and the season premieres alike, but let's also find joy in the interludes, the mid-season breaks, where life's narrative has room to breathe and we, its characters, have space to grow. After all, it's in these pauses that we often find the strength and insight to face the next set of cliffhangers.

• • •

As we conclude this chapter on the beauty of not trying, let us carry with us the gentle reminder that life, in its essence, is not a series of goals to be achieved but a rich tapestry of experiences to be lived. By embracing the philosophy of letting life happen, one binge at a time, we open ourselves to the full spectrum of human experience, finding joy, wonder, and sometimes enlightenment in the places we least expect. So, let's celebrate the art of not trying, not as a retreat from ambition, but as a path to a deeper, more meaningful engagement with the world around us. After all, in the serene landscape of contented existence, the true beauty of life unfolds in its own time, revealing that sometimes, the best way to find ourselves is simply to let go.

07

Social media scrolling – the pinnacle of modern achievement.

In the grand tapestry of contemporary milestones, where achievements are often measured by the tangible and the monumental, there emerges an unsung hero: social media scrolling. This modern-day odyssey, undertaken with the swipe of a finger, has quietly ascended to the pinnacle of everyday accomplishments. As we embark on this chapter, we'll explore the nuances of this digital voyage, navigating through the endless streams of content with the dexterity of seasoned explorers, and uncovering the hidden treasures of amusement, connection, and, occasionally, enlightenment.

In an age where the quest for productivity seems unending, the act of social media scrolling stands as a testament to the human capacity for curiosity and the desire for connection. It's a journey that begins with the intention of a brief respite, only to evolve into an expedition through the vast landscapes of human thought and creativity. Each scroll is a step forward, a dive deeper into the rabbit hole of information, entertainment, and sometimes, introspection. Here, amidst the cacophony of opinions, memes, and snapshots of life, we find a unique form of achievement: the mastery of content navigation, the art of engagement without exertion. This digital exploration offers a reprieve from the pressures of conventional productivity, allowing us to revel in the joy of discovery on our own terms. In the realm of social media, every like, share, and comment is a footprint left on the sands of the digital beach, marking our presence in the ever-expanding universe of online interaction. As we scroll, we're not just passing time; we're embarking on a journey of connection, learning, and sometimes, self-reflection, proving that achievement can indeed come in the most unexpected forms.

*C*onquer timelines, one scroll at a time – your thumb, the mightiest of warriors.

In the digital arena where endless timelines stretch before us, our thumbs emerge as the unsung heroes of the age, the silent warriors in the quiet battle of consumption and curation. As we embark on the daily scroll, these humble digits take on the weight of worlds, guiding us through the vast expanse of information with the precision of seasoned generals.

Conquering timelines is no small feat; it's an art form where strategy meets serendipity, each swipe a calculated step through the digital landscape. Our thumbs, tireless and unyielding, sift through the noise to find the signals, the nuggets of gold in a river of content. With each scroll, they weave through the tapestry of the now, curating a personal narrative from the threads of the global conversation. This journey through timelines is both a quest and a reflection, a way to engage with the world while also pausing to consider our place within it. In the grand scheme of things, these scrolls are more than just movements; they are expressions of choice, of agency in a world overflowing with voices. Our thumbs, in their silent dance, remind us of our power to shape our digital destinies, to choose which battles are worth fighting and which scrolls are worth following.

So, let us never underestimate the power of a well-aimed scroll, for in the kingdom of screens, the thumb is king, the mightiest of warriors in the subtle art of digital conquest.

In the quest for enlightenment, may your feed be endless and your battery, eternal.

As we journey through the digital expanse, seeking wisdom and connection in the glow of our screens, the quest for enlightenment takes on a new form. It's a voyage not through mountains and valleys but through endless feeds, where each swipe brings us closer to understanding, or so we hope.

In this modern odyssey, the feed becomes our map, a boundless scroll of insights, laughter, and the occasional cat video, leading us on a path to digital enlightenment. May our journey be unhampered by the mortal constraints of battery life, that our quest may continue uninterrupted by the physical limitations of our devices. As we navigate through the vastness of online wisdom, let the richness of shared human experience fuel our journey, transforming each post, tweet, and story into stepping stones towards greater knowledge. And as we delve deeper into the endless stream of content, let us find moments of true insight among the noise, gems of clarity that light our way. Amidst this expedition, may we never lose sight of the shore, remembering that enlightenment is not just found in the breadth of our feeds but in the depth of our engagement with the world around us.

So, as we embark on this endless scroll, may our batteries be as eternal as our thirst for knowledge, guiding us through the digital wilderness with unwavering light.

*A*scend the peaks of procrastination, where each like and share is a badge of honor.

In the vast landscape of modern-day tasks and responsibilities, there lies a mountain range more daunting than any physical summit: the peaks of procrastination. It's here that warriors of the digital age gather, not with ropes and picks, but with likes and shares as their tools of ascent.

Each step up these peaks is a dance with distraction, where the air is thick with the promise of 'just one more video' or 'one last scroll.' In this realm, every like is a declaration of solidarity, a nod to fellow climbers on their own journey of delay. Shares become the currency of camaraderie, a way to signal to those below that we, too, are champions of the cause, masters of the art of putting off until tomorrow what could surely be done today. As we ascend, the view from atop procrastination's pinnacle is both exhilarating and terrifying, offering a glimpse of all we've yet to do sprawled out beneath us in daunting clarity. Yet, in this moment of peak distraction, there's a peculiar pride in the badges of honor we've collected along the way—each like, each share, a testament to our ability to navigate the treacherous slopes of delay. It's here, on the summit, we realize that the journey through procrastination is not about the destination but about the stories we gather, the connections we make, and the artful dodge of productivity.

So, let us wear our likes and shares as medals of distinction, for in the kingdom of procrastination, they are the marks of true royalty, earned one glorious, unproductive step at a time.

• • •

So, as we close this chapter on social media scrolling, let us not underestimate the value of this modern pastime. In the art of scrolling, we find a reflection of our quest for knowledge, connection, and entertainment, proving that even in the simplest of actions, there can be a depth of accomplishment. As we navigate through our feeds, let us celebrate this digital voyage as a testament to our adaptability, our curiosity, and our unyielding pursuit of engagement in the digital age. After all, in the grand scheme of modern achievements, perhaps there's nothing more quintessentially contemporary than the mastery of the scroll.

08

Embracing the power of the snooze button – sleep as a form of protest against productivity.

In the relentless march towards productivity, where every moment is accounted for and every second is meant to be optimized, there lies a rebellious act so simple, yet so profound: hitting the snooze button. This chapter is an ode to the power of the snooze, a celebration of sleep not just as a biological necessity but as a form of protest against the productivity machine. It's a manifesto for those who choose to embrace the warmth of their bed a little longer, defying the early bird narrative and reclaiming rest as a radical act of self-preservation.

The snooze button, often vilified as the enemy of ambition, is, in fact, a bastion of resistance—a small, plastic herald of sanity in a world obsessed with doing more. Each press is a declaration of independence from the tyranny of the alarm clock, a deliberate choice to prioritize well-being over work, to value rest over hustle. In the act of snoozing, we acknowledge the absurdity of a culture that prizes exhaustion as a badge of honor, and we choose instead to champion our own health and happiness. This is not laziness; it's a strategic withdrawal from the battlefront of productivity, a momentary retreat to gather strength and embrace serenity. By valuing sleep as an act of protest, we challenge the narrative that our worth is measured by how much we can accomplish before dawn. Instead, we assert that in the quiet, in the extra ten minutes of slumber, we find a form of resistance that is both personal and profound. It's here, in the rebellious act of hitting snooze, that we reclaim our time, our energy, and our right to rest, setting boundaries against a world that demands our constant attention and effort.

*L*et every snooze be a silent rebellion against the dawn of productivity.

In the quiet hours of the morning, when the world whispers the call to action, there exists a simple, yet profound act of defiance: the hitting of the snooze button. It's a silent rebellion, a momentary refusal to bow to the relentless march of productivity that awaits us beyond the comfort of our beds.

With every press of that button, we declare our sovereignty over the start of our day, choosing serenity over the clamor of commitments. It's in these stolen moments of slumber that we find a rare peace, a respite from the demands of efficiency that will soon flood our waking hours. The snooze button becomes a shield, guarding the last remnants of our dreams from the intrusion of the day's obligations. It's a small act, yet it carries the weight of resistance, a daily reminder that in the battle between rest and productivity, there are victories to be found in the quiet corners of defiance. In this dance of delay, we reclaim a piece of ourselves, a fragment of freedom in the structured cadence of our lives. The act of snoozing is not just about seeking more rest; it's about asserting control, about making a choice in a day that will soon be filled with obligations that are not our own.

So, let every snooze be a testament to our resilience, a quiet battle cry in the dawn of productivity, reminding us that even in surrender, there is strength.

In the kingdom of slumber, the snooze button is your scepter, ruling over the morning's haste.

In the realm where dreams blend with reality, a kingdom governed by the gentle laws of slumber, there exists a symbol of power unlike any other: the snooze button. This modest device, unassuming in its appearance, holds the authority to command time, granting its wielder precious moments of rebellion against the dawn.

As the ruler of this tranquil domain, the snooze button serves as your scepter, an emblem of your sovereignty over the encroaching daylight and its demands. With each press, you enact a decree for silence, for the world to wait just a bit longer before claiming your consciousness. It's a magical instrument that pauses the march of productivity, allowing you to savor the warmth of your bed, the comfort of your pillow, and the weightlessness of dreams yet to fade. This scepter empowers you to stand at the threshold of waking life and decree, "Not yet," holding at bay the rush of tasks and toils for a few more moments of peace. In the kingdom of slumber, to snooze is to rule wisely, to understand the value of rest in a world that often forgets its worth. It's a daily act of self-care, a reminder that before we face the world, we must first tend to the realm within.

Thus, wield your scepter with confidence, for in the kingdom of slumber, the snooze button is not just a feature of your alarm; it's a declaration of your right to rest, to begin the day on your own terms.

Wage war on the morning alarm; your bed, the trench, and sleep, your ally in resistance.

In the early hours of each new day, a silent battlefield emerges from the comfort of our bedrooms, where the shrill call of the morning alarm marks the commencement of daily hostilities. Here, nestled within the sanctuary of sheets and pillows, lies the front line: our bed, transformed into a trench of resistance against the dawn's demands.

Armed with the blanket of determination and bolstered by the pillow of resolve, we enlist sleep as our most faithful ally, a comrade in arms in the struggle to reclaim the stolen moments of peace. Each snooze is a tactical maneuver, a deft retreat that strategizes for just a few minutes more in the embrace of dreams. The battle is waged not with weapons but with will, a test of endurance between the relentless siege of obligations and the fortitude of our desire for rest. It's here, in the soft stronghold of our beds, that we mount our defense, rallying the forces of slumber to hold the line against the advancing light. This war is not about victory in the traditional sense; it's about negotiation, about carving out a brief ceasefire in the relentless march of time. And in this daily conflict, our bed becomes more than just a place of rest; it's a bastion of rebellion, a testament to our right to pause, to breathe, to resist the hurry that awaits beyond its borders.

So, as the alarm sounds its battle cry, remember that your bed is your trench, and in the quiet defiance of sleep, there lies the power to withstand the morning's assault, one snooze at a time.

. . .

As we emerge from the shadows of our duvets, let us carry with us the power of the snooze, not as a sign of defiance but as a statement of self-care. In embracing sleep as a form of protest against productivity, we not only challenge the status quo but also advocate for a more balanced, humane approach to life—one where rest is not just permitted but celebrated. So, the next time the alarm rings, demanding you rise and join the ranks of the perpetually busy, remember that hitting snooze is not just an act of delaying the start of your day; it's a radical act of reclaiming your right to rest, to breathe, and to resist the relentless pace of productivity. After all, in a world that never sleeps, the truest form of rebellion is to dream.

09

The joy of canceled plans – the sweet, sweet sound of not having to socialize.

Ah, the modern-day symphony of a canceled plan—the unexpected melody that sings of free time reclaimed, of social batteries recharged without expenditure. This chapter is an anthem to the unsung joy of plans falling through, a celebration of the quiet bliss that comes with an evening suddenly, gloriously, empty. It's for those moments when the world expects you to step out, but fate hands you the gift of staying in. Here, we delve into why the sweet, sweet sound of not having to socialize isn't just a relief but a profound pleasure.

The joy of canceled plans is a multifaceted gem, sparkling with the allure of unscheduled time. It's the deep breath you didn't know you were holding, released at last when the text comes through:

"Can we take a rain check?" Suddenly, the evening stretches out like a blank canvas, ripe with potential for self-indulgence, relaxation, or perhaps, blissful nothingness. This joy is not rooted in aversion to others but in the love of one's own company, the rare and precious opportunity to be sovereign over one's time in an overbooked world. Each canceled plan is a reminder that sometimes, the best company is our own thoughts, our own quiet pursuits, free from the performative art of socialization. It's a moment to recalibrate, to turn inward, or simply to bask in the peace of our own space, undisturbed and unobligated. The unexpected joy of these moments teaches us the value of our own presence, the importance of rest, and the beauty of spontaneity—not in going out, but in staying in, embracing the sanctuary of solitude.

Celebrate the symphony of a silenced phone, where every canceled plan is a note of freedom.

In the crescendo of daily commitments and the cacophony of constant connectivity, there emerges a melody most sweet and unexpected: the symphony of a silenced phone, heralding the liberation of canceled plans. It's a rare composition, one that dances between the notes of obligation and the harmonies of spontaneity, crafting a tune that sings of freedom.

With every buzz that goes unanswered, every ring that fades into silence, we're gifted a measure of time reclaimed, a space in the score of our day where we are free to improvise. The canceled plans, each a note struck from the agenda, join together to form a melody of possibility, opening up a landscape of leisure previously obscured by the orchestrated performances of productivity. In this sudden quiet, we find the freedom to be, to breathe, to indulge in the art of doing nothing or the joy of doing something unplanned. It's in these moments, these pauses between the movements of our lives, that we rediscover the beauty of unscheduled time, the luxury of living at our own rhythm. The symphony of a silenced phone becomes not a sign of missed connections but a celebration of connection to oneself, an ode to the personal peace that comes from stepping off the stage, if only for a moment.

So, let us revel in the unexpected quiet, the sudden stillness that canceled plans afford, and find within it the notes of freedom to compose our own symphony of serenity.

In the quiet of unscheduled evenings, find bliss in the company of your own solitude.

In the hustle of day-to-day life, where schedules dictate our every move and time is a currency spent with meticulous care, the arrival of an unscheduled evening unfolds like a rare treasure map. It beckons with the promise of uncharted bliss, a journey into the heart of solitude where the only companion is the self.

As the sun dips below the horizon, casting long shadows that whisper of stillness, this unscheduled time becomes a sanctuary. It's an invitation to wander through the corridors of your own thoughts, to dance with your shadows, and to embrace the quiet that so often eludes us. Here, in the company of your solitude, you're free to explore the vast landscapes within, to rediscover forgotten dreams and to sit with the parts of yourself that clamor for attention in the din of daily life. This bliss is not born of isolation but of reconnection, a return to the core of who you are, unencumbered by the expectations and demands of the world outside. It's in these moments of solitude that we often find our truest selves, learning to enjoy our own company as much as we do others'. The unscheduled evening becomes a canvas, and your solitude, the brush with which you paint moments of introspection, relaxation, and profound peace.

Embrace the quiet of unscheduled evenings as an opportunity to befriend your solitude, discovering within it a bliss that is uniquely and wonderfully yours.

Revel in the unexpected gift of time, unwrapped with each message of regretful cancellation.

In the intricate dance of social obligations and personal commitments, the unexpected message of cancellation arrives not as a disappointment, but as a gift—a parcel of time suddenly bestowed upon us, wrapped in the guise of changed plans. It's a moment of serendipity, offering a pause in the relentless rhythm of our days.

Each message of regret, each polite note of apology for plans unfulfilled, becomes an invitation to step back and breathe. It's a chance to diverge from the scripted path of our day-to-day, to explore the quiet corners of time we often overlook. This newfound freedom is a canvas, once filled with the ink of others' expectations, now blank and awaiting your touch. Here, in the open spaces carved out by canceled plans, we find the liberty to pursue whims left on the wayside, to indulge in self-care long deferred, or simply to savor the sweetness of doing nothing at all. This unexpected gift of time asks nothing of us but to be enjoyed, to be used in whatever manner brings us joy or peace. It's a reminder that sometimes, the best moments in life are those that arrive unannounced, wrapped in the simplicity of an open schedule.

So, revel in these moments, unwrapping each with the excitement of possibility, for in every cancellation lies the opportunity to rediscover the joys of unscheduled freedom.

• • •

As we close this chapter, let's carry forward the lesson of the canceled plan — not as a disappointment, but as an unexpected gift. Let us find joy in the quiet, in the unstructured moments that life, in its unpredictable wisdom, occasionally offers. The next time a plan falls through, let's listen for the sweet, sweet sound of freedom it brings, a melody that sings of possibilities unbound by social commitments. After all, in the rush and rumble of our busy lives, the joy of canceled plans is a gentle reminder that sometimes, the best place to be is exactly where we are — comfortably ensconced in our own delightful company.

10

Why make your bed when you're just going to sleep in it again?

In the grand theater of daily rituals and routines, one act often stands out as particularly perplexing: the making of one's bed. This chapter ponders the curious habit of tidying up something that's destined to be undone just hours later. It's a humorous look at the Sisyphean task that begins each day, questioning the logic behind smoothing sheets and fluffing pillows when, inevitably, we're just going to sleep in it again. Let's dive into the comforting tangle of reasons why leaving the bed unmade might not just be laziness, but a small act of rebellion against the mundane.

The ritual of making the bed each morning is touted as a cornerstone of discipline, a small victory to set the tone for the day. Yet, there's a certain liberation in asking, "Why bother?" Each morning presents a choice: to spend those precious moments wrestling with bed linens or to embrace the day's potential unencumbered by such trivialities. The unmade bed stands as a testament to our humanity, a reminder that not all aspects of life need be perfectly curated to be meaningful. It's a silent protest against the pressure to appear perpetually put-together, an acknowledgment that some messes, like our own internal ones, are just part of being human. This isn't an endorsement of disorder, but an invitation to prioritize—to consider whether the aesthetic appeal of a neatly made bed is worth more than a few extra moments of sleep or contemplation. In the grand scheme, the state of our beds speaks less to our character than our ability to discern which tasks truly merit our time and energy.

Embrace the eternal cycle of unrested sheets; today's creases are tomorrow's comfort.

In the quiet theater of the everyday, where the mundane becomes the stage for life's little dramas, there exists a cycle as constant as the moon's dance with the night: the eternal cycle of unrested sheets. Each morning, we rise, leaving behind a landscape of creases and folds—a testament to the night's restlessness or its tender embrace.

These creases, though often seen as a sign of disarray, are in fact the marks of life lived fully, of dreams chased through the corridors of sleep. They speak to the comfort found in the familiar, the softness that comes not from perfection but from use, from the accumulation of nights spent wrapped in thought, in dreams, or in the warmth of loved ones. As we smooth the sheets each morning, we erase the imprints of yesterday, preparing the canvas for the night to come. Yet, it's in the anticipation of returning to these sheets, to the comfort of their embrace, that we find a simple joy. The cycle of making and unmaking the bed is not just a chore but a ritual, a reminder of the passage of time and the rhythm of life. Today's creases become tomorrow's comfort, a promise that no matter what the day brings, the sanctuary of our bed awaits, ready to wrap us in the familiarity of its unrested embrace.

So, let us embrace the eternal cycle of unrested sheets, finding beauty in the imperfection and comfort in the creases that tell the story of our nights.

In the art of living, a messy bed is a masterpiece painted daily with the strokes of rest.

Within the gallery of daily life, where each action paints its mark on the canvas of existence, there lies a quiet masterpiece often overlooked: the messy bed. This disheveled tableau, far from being a sign of neglect, is a work of art created by the most human of experiences—rest.

Every twisted sheet and crumpled pillowcase is a stroke of authenticity, a physical manifestation of the body's journey through the realm of sleep. These are the brushstrokes of comfort, the lines drawn by moments of turning and dreaming, each crease a testament to the night's embrace. The art of living is not found in pristine, untouched canvases but in the ones marked by our presence, our movements, our lives. A messy bed represents a space lived in and loved, a space where weariness finds solace and the soul finds renewal. It is a daily masterpiece, ever-changing, painted with the most delicate and personal of brushes— ourselves. In this artwork, we see not disarray but the beauty of living fully, of embracing each day and night with the entirety of our being.

Thus, let us view our messy beds not as tasks to be tidied but as masterpieces to be appreciated, for in the art of living, they are vivid reminders of our humanity, painted daily with the strokes of rest.

*R*esist the tyranny of tidiness; let your bed be a sanctuary of lived-in peace.

In the realm of domestic existence, where order often reigns supreme and the visuals of tidiness are equated with virtue, there emerges a call to arms—or rather, a call to ease. It's a gentle rebellion against the tyranny of an always-tidy bed, advocating for the space within our sheets to be a sanctuary of lived-in peace.

This resistance is not a denial of cleanliness or order but an embrace of comfort and authenticity. The bed, with its tumbled sheets and pillows askew, becomes a testament to the moments of rest and repose it has granted us. Each wrinkle in the fabric, a silent witness to the dreams and deep breaths of the night's quiet hours. In this space, we find not chaos but the traces of our presence, the echoes of our relaxation. It's here, in the gentle disorder of our bedding, that we allow ourselves a momentary reprieve from the world's demands for constant perfection. This sanctuary of lived-in peace offers us a reminder that it's okay to leave some corners of our lives unpolished, to find beauty in the imperfections that make us human. By resisting the urge to straighten every sheet and fluff every pillow, we claim a small victory for our well-being, honoring the need for spaces that reflect the reality of our lives, not the idealized versions often sought after.

So, let us resist the tyranny of tidiness, allowing our beds—and by extension, our lives—to be beautifully imperfect sanctuaries of lived-in peace, where the only expectation is rest.

. . .

As we tuck this chapter away, let's reconsider the unmade bed not as a sign of disarray, but as a symbol of our capacity to choose our battles. In questioning why we make our beds only to unmake them each night, we uncover broader truths about the rituals and routines that shape our lives. Perhaps, in the end, the choice to leave the bed unmade is a small declaration of independence, a way to claim a bit more freedom in a world obsessed with order. So, the next time you contemplate the creases in your sheets, remember that it's not just about the bed—it's about questioning the "whys" of our daily lives and, sometimes, allowing ourselves to leave things as they are, perfectly imperfect.

11

Diet starts tomorrow – the mantra of eternal postponement.

D iet starts tomorrow – a phrase as familiar as it is fraught with the echoes of deferred hopes and culinary indulgences. This chapter delves into the deliciously deceptive world of eternal postponement, where intentions are as rich as the desserts deferred for the sake of a slimmer tomorrow. It's a humorous exploration of the cyclical dance between aspiration and gratification, a look at why we so often set our sights on a healthier horizon, only to find ourselves anchored in the comforting harbor of today's treats.

The mantra of "diet starts tomorrow" serves as both a shield and a saboteur, a way to justify today's indulgences with promises of tomorrow's restraint. It's a temporal bargain, where the currency is willpower and the exchange rate is always in favor of the present. This recurring postponement isn't just about food; it's a reflection of our complex relationship with self-control, desire, and the human tendency to prefer immediate joy over future benefits. Each time we utter this mantra, we acknowledge our intentions to change, even as we embrace the comfort of familiar habits. It's a dance of delay, where the music never stops and the steps are all too familiar. Yet, there's a beauty in this cycle, a shared humanity in the struggle between what we aspire to be and what we are in the moment. The phrase becomes a symbol of our perpetual optimism, a testament to our belief in fresh starts and new beginnings, regardless of how many times we've circled this track.

*F**east today, for tomorrow's diet is but a distant promise on the horizon of indulgence.*

In the grand banquet of life, where every choice is a dish served on the table of consequence, there emerges a timeless decree: Feast today. This pronouncement is not one of recklessness, but a celebration of the moment, a recognition of the fleeting nature of our desires and the joys they bring.

Today's feast is an act of liberation, a bold embrace of pleasure over restraint, where the savoring of each bite is a testament to the richness of the present. It's a reminder that the strictures of tomorrow's diet belong to a future yet to unfold, a distant shore on the horizon of indulgence that need not concern us now. In this moment, we are invited to revel in the abundance before us, to indulge in the flavors and experiences that life offers with open hands. This feast is a declaration of our right to enjoy, to taste the sweetness and the complexity of the world without the shadow of tomorrow's judgement. It's in this space of permission that we find a deeper appreciation for the art of living fully, for recognizing that denial has its place, but so does delight. The promise of a diet tomorrow is not a sentence but a gentle acknowledgement that balance is a dance, and today, the music calls for celebration.

So, let us feast today, with hearts light and spirits unburdened, for the morrow's restraint is but a whisper on the wind, and today, the banquet of life is rich and waiting.

In the calendar of self-improvement, 'tomorrow' is a recurring day of hopeful beginnings.

In the vast expanse of self-growth and personal development, where aspirations tower like mountains and ambitions stretch like the endless sea, there exists a peculiar phenomenon: the ever-renewing promise of 'tomorrow.' It's a day marked not by the sun's rise and set but by the perpetual yearning for a fresh start, a clean slate on which to etch the dreams deferred and the goals yet to be pursued.

This 'tomorrow' is a beacon of hope in the calendar of self-improvement, a recurring reminder that the journey towards betterment is never linear, nor does it heed the strictures of time. Each iteration of 'tomorrow' brings with it the possibility of transformation, the potential for change that keeps the flame of optimism alight. It's a testament to the human spirit's resilience, to our innate capacity to rise from the ashes of today's shortcomings with a renewed vigor for the challenges ahead. In this cycle of hopeful beginnings, we find not just the promise of progress but the acceptance of imperfection, an understanding that growth is a mosaic of attempts, successes, and setbacks. 'Tomorrow' becomes not just a day in the future but a symbol of our commitment to ourselves, a pledge to continue striving, learning, and evolving. It's in this space of perpetual renewal that we truly engage with the art of self-improvement, embracing each 'tomorrow' as an opportunity to be better than we were the day before.

So, let us welcome each 'tomorrow' with open arms and hopeful hearts, for in the calendar of self-improvement, it is the most precious day of all, ever-present and brimming with the potential for new beginnings.

Savor the present; tomorrow's restraint is just another dessert away.

In the grand feast of life, where each moment is a dish to be savored and each decision a flavor on the tongue, there exists a delicate balance between indulgence and restraint. It's a dance as old as time, where the present offers itself up as a banquet of immediate delights, and tomorrow waits in the wings, a course of moderation yet to be served.

Today invites us to relish in its richness, to sink our teeth into the succulence of now, unburdened by the diet of denial that tomorrow promises. It's in this celebration of the present that we find the sweetness of being truly alive, tasting each experience as if it were the finest chocolate, melting away to memories. Tomorrow's restraint, though looming, becomes just another dessert on the menu of choices, a potential selection in the endless buffet of life's options. In choosing to savor the present, we acknowledge that the joy of living is not found in the abstinence of pleasure but in the mindful enjoyment of it. This moment, ripe with possibility, reminds us that while the future may require moderation, today is ours to feast upon with gusto. The art of savoring the present teaches us that life, in all its fleeting beauty, is a series of dishes to be enjoyed, not merely endured.

So, let us toast to the now, for tomorrow's restraint is indeed just another dessert away, and today offers an abundance of flavors too rich to ignore.

• • •

As we wrap up our feast of thoughts on the mantra "diet starts tomorrow," let's savor the sweetness of understanding and self-compassion. This phrase, often repeated with a mix of humor and resignation, is less an admission of defeat than a celebration of our perpetual optimism. It reminds us that every day offers a new opportunity for change, even if we choose to embrace that change "tomorrow." So, the next time you find yourself reaching for that extra slice of cake with a promise of dietary redemption on the horizon, remember that the journey toward self-improvement isn't a straight line. It's a winding path filled with detours, delays, and delicious diversions. And perhaps, in the grand scheme of things, that's perfectly okay.

12

Procrastination as a lifestyle – why do today what you can indefinitely postpone?

In the high-speed highway of life, where productivity and efficiency are the engines that drive us forward, there exists a scenic bypath known as procrastination. This chapter is an ode to the art of delaying, a light-hearted exploration of procrastination not just as a habit but as a lifestyle choice. It's a celebration of the decision to say, "Why do today what can be delightfully postponed?"—a question that champions the joy of living in the moment, even if that moment is artfully stretched to its limits.

Procrastination as a lifestyle is the embodiment of embracing the present, a philosophy that prioritizes the pleasures of now over the potential toils of later. It's a conscious choice to live at a pace dictated not by deadlines but by one's own rhythms and whims. This isn't to say that procrastinators lack ambition or direction; rather, they possess a unique skill in balancing urgency with tranquility, understanding that not all tasks require immediate action, and that some moments are better spent in the pursuit of leisure or creative idleness. The art of indefinite postponement is not about avoidance but about allocation—choosing where to direct one's energies in a way that maximizes joy and minimizes stress. It's a form of rebellion against the societal pressure to always be "on," a gentle reminder that time is not just a resource to be optimized but a gift to be enjoyed. In this world, deadlines are flexible, schedules are suggestions, and the to-do list is less a commandment and more a gentle guideline.

Today's tasks are tomorrow's adventures; embrace the thrill of the last-minute quest.

In the grand narrative of life, where each day is a page in our unwritten saga, the tasks we set aside today become the seeds of tomorrow's adventures. It's a perspective that transforms the mundane into the magical, the procrastinated into the promising. As we stand at the threshold of today, gazing into the horizon of tomorrow, we're not merely delaying; we're setting the stage for a tale of last-minute quests and thrilling escapades.

These tasks, once seen as burdens to be borne, morph into challenges that call to our inner adventurer, beckoning us with the siren song of the eleventh hour. The thrill of the last-minute quest lies not in the task itself but in the journey it inspires—a dash against time, a race against the setting sun. It's in these moments, with the clock as our nemesis and adrenaline as our ally, that we discover our true capacity for creativity, resourcefulness, and determination. Each delayed task becomes a dragon to be slain, a mountain to be climbed, a chasm to be leaped across in the daring dance of accomplishment. The anticipation of the adventure lends a certain sweetness to the procrastination, a promise that when the time comes, we will rise to the occasion, swords drawn and hearts alight. And so, as we navigate the landscape of our to-do lists, let us not see them as mere tasks but as invitations to embark on quests that await our heroism.

Thus, let us embrace the thrill of the last-minute quest, for in the heart of every procrastinator beats the soul of an adventurer, ready to transform today's tasks into tomorrow's legendary exploits.

Master the art of tomorrow; let each day be a canvas for potential, not immediate action.

In the rich tapestry of existence, where each day unfolds as a fresh canvas, there exists a profound artistry in the embrace of tomorrow. This isn't about neglect or avoidance but about viewing time as a medium for potential, a space where the seeds of future actions are sown with thoughtful intention. As we stand before the dawn of each new day, we are not pressured artists rushed to complete our masterpiece but thoughtful creators who understand the value of patience and the promise of what lies ahead.

The art of mastering tomorrow lies in recognizing that not all must be accomplished today, that the

.

true beauty of potential is in its unfolding. Each day offers itself as a canvas not cluttered with the hurried strokes of immediate action but adorned with the deliberate marks of considered planning. In this space, we grant ourselves the permission to dream, to plot, and to envision the steps that will lead us to our goals, understanding that the masterpiece of our lives is composed over time, not in a single frenzied session. This approach allows us to breathe, to live in the present while gently guiding our focus toward the horizon of tomorrow. It's a dance between action and contemplation, where the artistry comes not from the flurry of activity but from the graceful balance of knowing when to act and when to pause. In mastering the art of tomorrow, we cultivate a sense of peace with the pace of our progress, trusting that each day's potential, when fully embraced, leads to a richer, more nuanced journey.

So, let us approach each day as a canvas for potential, not immediate action, and in doing so, master the art of tomorrow, painting our lives with the thoughtful strokes of time well considered.

In the garden of time, procrastination is the seed that blooms at the eleventh hour.

In the lush, verdant expanse of our lives, where the passage of time is both gardener and terrain, there grows a peculiar flora: procrastination. Often seen as a weed rather than a blossom, it nonetheless has its season of bloom, revealing its true colors in the waning light of the eleventh hour. This is not a plant of idleness but one of latent potential, waiting for the precise moment to unfold.

The garden of time is tended not just with the diligent care of constant activity but with the patience to let certain seeds germinate in their own rhythm. Procrastination, the seed sown deep within this garden, lies dormant not out of reluctance but in anticipation of the right conditions for growth. It flourishes under the pressure of deadlines, thriving in the adrenaline-rich soil of last-minute efforts. This unexpected bloom, often criticized for its timing, brings with it a burst of creativity and efficiency that can only emerge under the unique stress of impending finality. It's in these pressured moments that procrastination reveals its purpose, not as a barrier to productivity, but as a catalyst for focused action. The eleventh hour is not just a marker of time running out but a signal for this seed to break through the surface, transforming procrastination from a mere delay into a strategic pause, a period of gathering strength for the final, decisive push.

Thus, in the garden of time, let us not hastily uproot the seed of procrastination, for it too has its place and purpose, blooming beautifully at the eleventh hour when the conditions are just right.

• • •

As we close this chapter on procrastination as a lifestyle, let's carry with us a newfound appreciation for the gentle art of delay. It's a reminder that in the rush to accomplish and achieve, there's also value in pausing, in breathing, and in allowing ourselves the freedom to explore life at our own pace. So, the next time you find yourself putting off a task for another day, remember that procrastination isn't just a habit— it's a choice, a way of embracing the present with open arms and a relaxed smile. After all, why rush through life when you can saunter through it, taking in the sights and sounds at a pace that lets you truly appreciate them? In the end, maybe it's not about doing more but about enjoying more, one postponed task at a time.

13

The illusion of potential – keeping hopes low to avoid disappointment.

In the vast landscape of human emotion, where hopes soar like eagles and dreams stretch towards the horizon, there exists a pragmatic strategy often mistaken for cynicism: the careful calibration of expectations to avoid the sting of disappointment. This chapter explores the nuanced art of maintaining low expectations, not as a testament to a lack of ambition, but as a sophisticated defense mechanism against the inevitable vicissitudes of life. It's an examination of the illusion of potential, a reminder that sometimes, the most prudent path to contentment is paved with the stones of modest hopes.

The philosophy of keeping hopes low is akin to sailing on the sea of life with a well-anchored boat; it's about preparing for storms while still appreciating the beauty of the voyage. This approach acknowledges the dual nature of potential: while it inspires us to reach for the stars, it also sets the stage for possible descent into the valleys of disappointment. By tempering our expectations, we navigate these waters with a seasoned sailor's wisdom, knowing that while not every venture will lead to treasure, the journey itself holds value. This doesn't mean shutting the door on aspiration or joy; rather, it's about embracing a realistic perspective that finds beauty in the attainable, satisfaction in the simple, and a deep sense of peace in the acceptance of life's unpredictable tides. It's a delicate balance, this dance with potential, one that requires both the courage to dream and the wisdom to hold those dreams lightly. In doing so, we protect ourselves from the harsher blows of disillusionment, finding solace in the small victories and the quiet joys that dot the landscape of our lives.

*N*avigate life's expectations like a limbo bar; the lower you go, the easier to pass.

In the intricate dance of existence, where life's expectations stretch taut across our path like the bar in a limbo game, there's a strategy as graceful as it is pragmatic: the lower we set the bar, the easier we find it to pass beneath. This isn't a counsel for underachievement but a playful acknowledgment of the flexibility required to navigate the expectations set before us.

As we approach each new challenge, the metaphorical limbo bar of expectations looms, demanding a contortion of spirit and intent. To lower this bar is not to admit defeat but to recognize the power of adaptability, the strength found in acknowledging our limits while still engaging in the game. With each bend and twist, we learn more about our resilience, our capacity to move through life with a nimbleness that defies the rigid postures of perfection. This dance beneath life's expectations teaches us that success is not always about clearing the highest bar but about moving forward, maintaining balance and grace under the weight of our ambitions. In this way, lowering the bar becomes a strategy for progress, a method by which we measure advancement not by the height of our achievements but by the depth of our journey. And so, as we limbo beneath the ever-changing heights of expectation, we discover that the true victory lies in the fluid motion of passage, in the joy found in the movement itself.

Thus, let us navigate life's expectations like a limbo bar, understanding that sometimes, the lower we go, the easier it is to pass, and in this passage, find the freedom to dance through life with ease and joy.

In the economy of hope, invest minimally to ensure the dividends of contentment.

In the vast marketplace of emotions, where hope is both currency and commodity, there lies a strategy as prudent as it is profound: the minimal investment of hope to ensure the steady dividends of contentment. This approach is not born of cynicism but of a seasoned understanding of the delicate balance between desire and fulfillment, between the soaring heights of expectation and the grounding reality of life's outcomes.

By investing our hope with caution, we temper the risks associated with overextension, guarding against the sharp sting of disappointment that often follows unchecked optimism. This careful allocation of our emotional resources allows us to appreciate the value of what is, rather than mourning the absence of what might have been. It's a strategy that cultivates resilience, teaching us to find joy in the simple, the immediate, and the attainable. In doing so, we build a portfolio of contentment, diversified not by the pursuit of elusive highs but by the steady accumulation of life's small pleasures and victories. This minimal investment in hope does not diminish our capacity for joy but enhances it, enabling us to savor the returns of contentment with a heart unburdened by the debts of unmet expectations. It's in this economy of hope that we learn the art of emotional investment, where the wisdom of restraint brings the wealth of peace.

Thus, in the economy of hope, let us invest minimally, ensuring that the dividends of contentment enrich our lives with a wealth not of what could be, but of what is, fostering a richness of spirit grounded in the joy of the present.

Cultivate a garden of modest dreams, where the fruits of reality are always within reach.

In the fertile soil of aspiration, where dreams grow wild and unruly, guided by the boundless imagination of our inner landscape, there exists a tranquil plot: the garden of modest dreams. This is not a lesser plot by any means, but a deliberate cultivation of desires that stand firmly within the grasp of possibility. It's a testament to the understanding that not all dreams need to tower like redwoods, stretching beyond the clouds of reality.

In this garden, each dream is planted with care, chosen for its ability to thrive in the climate of the actual, watered with the patience of practicality. Here, the fruits of reality are not bitter with the taste of compromise but sweet with the satisfaction of attainment. This cultivation of modest dreams does not stem from a fear of reaching too high but from the wisdom of knowing the value of each step taken, of appreciating the journey as much as the destination. The beauty of this garden lies in its accessibility, in the way its paths invite us to wander, hands brushing against the tangible, the achievable. In tending to this plot, we learn that dreams, like plants, flourish best when given the right conditions for growth—not in the shadow of the unattainable, but in the sunlight of the possible. The garden of modest dreams becomes a sanctuary, a space where the seeds of ambition meet the nurturing ground of reality, growing into a landscape where every dream has the chance to bloom.

Thus, let us cultivate our garden of modest dreams, where the fruits of reality are always within reach, and discover the profound joy in harvesting the attainable, in celebrating the beauty of dreams that grow not into the sky, but into our lives.

• • •

As we conclude our reflection on the illusion of potential and the strategy of low expectations, let's consider the possibility that this approach, far from being defeatist, is a form of emotional intelligence—a way to navigate the highs and lows of existence with grace and equilibrium. By keeping our hopes at a gentle simmer, we're not limiting our capacity for happiness; we're ensuring that our happiness is not held hostage by the whims of fate. In the end, the art of managing expectations is not about dimming the light of potential but about illuminating the path to a more serene and grounded life, where disappointment is a rare visitor, and contentment a constant companion.

14

The pursuit of average – why excel when you can blend in?

In a world that constantly celebrates the outliers, the overachievers, and the extraordinary, there's a quiet but significant space for the pursuit of average. This chapter is a homage to the understated beauty of blending in, a thoughtful exploration of why excelling isn't always the goal. It's an invitation to appreciate the calm waters of mediocrity, where the pressures of greatness give way to the gentle currents of contentment. Here, we delve into the rationale behind choosing a path that's not about reaching the peak but about enjoying the journey at a steady, comfortable pace.

The pursuit of average is not a surrender to complacency but a conscious choice to embrace balance. In the equilibrium of the ordinary, there's a freedom from the relentless race for recognition, a liberation from the weight of expectation. This isn't about shunning ambition but about redefining success on one's own terms, recognizing that life's worth isn't measured by the height of one's achievements but by the depth of one's satisfaction. Here, in the realm of the average, we find a community of like-minded souls who appreciate the fine art of living without the need for applause. This collective journey celebrates the individual for who they are, not what they accomplish, fostering an environment where the pressure to stand out is replaced by the comfort of fitting in. It's in this space that we can truly relax, unburdened by the need to constantly prove ourselves, free to pursue interests not for accolades but for the pure joy they bring. The pursuit of average, then, is not a path to mediocrity but a road to self-acceptance, where the true measure of success is personal happiness and well-being.

*I*n the chorus of life, there's harmony in being another voice, not always the solo.

In the grand symphony of existence, where every individual's story weaves into the larger narrative of humanity, there exists a profound beauty in the chorus—a collective harmony that resonates with the shared experiences of many. To be a voice among others, to blend rather than stand apart, is not a diminishment of one's unique melody but an embrace of the communal song of life.

The chorus teaches us that there is strength in unity, that our voices, when joined with others, create a music more complex and beautiful than any solo could achieve. It's in this ensemble that we find comfort in commonality, a sense of belonging that comes from sharing the stage of existence. Being part of the chorus allows us to contribute to something greater than ourselves, to be a part of a melody that stretches across time and space, touching lives and echoing through generations. It reminds us that our individual stories, while singular, gain depth and meaning when sung in harmony with others. The chorus is not about losing one's voice but about finding it within the weave of humanity, understanding that sometimes, the most profound impact is made not by standing alone but by standing together. In the chorus of life, each voice matters, each contribution adds to the richness of the whole, teaching us that in the grand scheme of things, harmony is not just a musical concept but a blueprint for living.

Thus, let us cherish our place in the chorus of life, recognizing the harmony in being another voice, where our melodies find strength and beauty not in solitude but in the symphony of shared existence.

Why climb the mountain when the view from the base camp is comfortably satisfactory?

In the vast landscape of ambition, where peaks of achievement beckon with their siren call, there lies a gentle question, softly spoken yet profound in its simplicity: Why climb the mountain when the view from the base camp is comfortably satisfactory?

It's an inquiry that challenges the relentless pursuit of higher, further, faster, urging us to pause and consider the beauty of contentment found in the here and now.

The base camp, with its unassuming vantage point, offers a perspective rich in its own right, a panorama of life's journey that doesn't require the perilous ascent to appreciate. From this vantage, the mountain remains a symbol of possibility, yet the choice to climb is ours alone, free from the compulsion of conquest. It's here, in the embrace of the base camp's comfort, that we find permission to savor the accomplishments already achieved, to bask in the satisfaction of journeys completed rather than constantly seeking new horizons. This isn't about eschewing ambition but about recognizing the value in the paths we've already traversed, the lessons learned, and the beauty witnessed along the way. The base camp invites us to reflect on our own definitions of success, to understand that sometimes, the greatest achievements are not found at the summit but in the ability to find joy in the journey, regardless of its altitude. In questioning the need to climb, we open ourselves to the possibility that perhaps, contentment lies not in the endless pursuit of the next peak but in the appreciation of the ground beneath our feet.

So, let us ponder the value of the base camp's view, finding in its comfortable satisfaction a reminder that sometimes, the most fulfilling path is the one that allows us to simply be, to live fully in the moment, surrounded by the beauty of the mountains we choose to climb or simply admire from afar.

*E**mbrace the middle road, where expectations are gentle and the journey is unassuming.*

In the vast expanse of life's journey, where paths diverge towards peaks of ambition and valleys of simplicity, there exists a middle road—a path less celebrated yet rich with the promise of balance. This route does not seek the extremes but finds beauty in moderation, a space where expectations are gentle, and the pace of progress is measured not by the milestones passed but by the quality of the journey itself.

The middle road is an invitation to slow down, to appreciate the scenery that the race for achievement often blurs. It's a path where success is defined not by reaching distant horizons but by the depth of the experiences gathered along the way. Here, the pressure to excel is replaced by the permission to explore, to grow at one's own pace without the shadow of comparison darkening the way. This road teaches us the value of presence, of being fully engaged with the unfolding of life in its myriad forms, without the constant gaze towards the next achievement. The journey becomes unassuming, marked by a series of small joys and discoveries that, in their accumulation, create a tapestry of fulfillment that the pursuit of extremes often misses. On this path, the traveler finds contentment in the equilibrium between striving and being, learning that the greatest treasures are often found not at the destination but in the moments of quiet contemplation along the way.

Thus, let us embrace the middle road, where the journey is marked by gentle expectations and an unassuming pace, discovering in its balance a profound freedom to experience life in all its nuanced beauty.

. . .

As we wrap up our exploration of the pursuit of average, let's carry forward the understanding that there's profound strength in choosing contentment over competition. In a society that often equates worth with achievement, choosing to blend in is a form of quiet rebellion, a statement that one's value is intrinsic and not dependent on external validation. So, the next time you find yourself caught in the whirlwind of comparison, remember the serenity that comes with the pursuit of average —a serenity born of self-acceptance, balance, and the profound realization that sometimes, being just fine is more than enough. After all, in the vast tapestry of human experience, it's not the bright colors that always draw the eye but the subtle shades that create depth and harmony.

15
Outro

A s we close the book on our voyage through "The Art of Underachievement – Embracing Mediocrity in a World Obsessed with Success," we stand on the brink of newfound insight. From this perspective, we witness life unfold, welcoming the ordinary with open arms, finding a subtle joy in the modest troughs of mediocrity over the towering summits of excellence.

Our journey has been one of intentional pace, relishing the aroma of projects left dangling and the rough edges of dreams not fully formed. We've moved to the leisurely tempo of delay, found a sweet spot in being just average, and let the soft flow of directionlessness chart our path. This trek has shown us that true wisdom doesn't chase after glory but wraps itself in the comfort of the everyday, that happiness blooms in the terrain of tempered hopes, and that acknowledging our own boundaries reveals a deep-seated resilience. This narrative hasn't been about forsaking aspirations but about adjusting our sails on the seas of success, seeking equilibrium in a world that measures value by accomplishments, and understanding that the most profound rebellion may just be in accepting our adequacy as our best.

Thus, as you turn the final page, may the echoes of its message linger. May you revel in the unassuming beauty of routine, find vigor in acknowledging your perfectly average self, and discover serenity in the knowledge that life's tapestry is richest not in the epic sagas of victory but in the quiet stories of satisfied underperformance. Remember, in the craft of underachieving, each serene moment is a triumph, each ordinary day a work of art. Here's to a life celebrated in shades of the ordinary, to a spirit freed from the insatiable hunger for more, and to uncovering the remarkable in the folds of the beautifully mundane.

Maxwell Easeley

Made in United States
Troutdale, OR
05/10/2024

19782964R00066